STIPPLE, WINK
AND GUSSET

STIPPLE, WINK AND GUSSET

JAMES COCHRANE

CENTURY
London Sydney Auckland Johannesburg

Published in 1992 by Century
Random Century Limited
20 Vauxhall Bridge Road
London SW1V 2SA

Random Century Australia (Pty) Ltd
20 Alfred Street, Milsons Point, Sydney,
NSW 2061 Australia

Random Century New Zealand Ltd
PO Box 40-086, Glenfield, Auckland 10
New Zealand

Random Century South Africa (Pty) Ltd
PO Box 337, Berglvei, 2012 South Africa

ISBN 0 7126 5573 5

Designed and typeset by Roger Walker

Printed and bound in Great Britain by
Butler & Tanner Ltd, Frome and London

*The author wishes to thank
Dover Publications for the use of
seventeen illustrations from* Trades
and Occupations, (*1990*), *edited by
Carol Belanger Grafton*

FOREWORD

SOME YEARS ago, while browsing in an old volume
of naval history, I came upon the poignant tale of
Captain Frederick Doldrum. Curious, for the story
was new to me, I had recourse to my dictionary, to
see how it might have summarized his career. The
word 'doldrums' was there, of course, but, surpris-
ingly, with no mention whatsoever of the gallant
but unfortunate gentleman who had given it to our
English language. Some days later I had exactly the
same experience after I had stumbled upon an
anecdote concerning Lieutenant Edward Awning in
the same volume. Again, the word was there, but
not the man. My otherwise reliable – or so I then
believed – dictionary paid proper homage (the *mot
juste*, I think) to Joseph Hansom, of cab fame (of
which more later, however), and to the ill-starred
Captain Boycott, and to Mrs Bloomer, and to
numerous other eponyms. But Doldrum and
Awning had somehow slipped through the lexico-
graphical, or rather the etymological, net.

Idly, but only for a moment or two, I wondered
how many others, worthy or unworthy, had suffered the same fate, but I put the matter out of my

mind as unimportant in the larger scheme of things. It was only some months later, when an art historian friend casually mentioned the American painter Henry George Stipple, and I had the impulse to look the word 'stipple' up – and again found it quite unattributed – that I began to think that something was amiss. I purchased other, supposedly better, dictionaries. I read through them in an entirely new light. I spot-checked them for eponyms I already knew. Good Heavens! Akimbo was not there, nor Ricochet (though no doubt if he *had* killed Lord Nelson he would have been), nor even the redoubtable Sir Oswald Binge (an ancestor of my own family). Clearly something was *badly* amiss.

I can remember clearly the moment when I resolved to enter upon the quest of which this little book is the result. I was enjoying a brief holiday in Paris, and, as is my wont, spent an afternoon wandering among the evocative tombs of the cemetery of Père Lachaise, where the bones of so many of the famous, and the infamous, lie. Following one of the alleys that I had possibly not trodden since I first went there as a boy, I suddenly found myself reading the epitaph, incised upon a fine and moving equestrian statue, of Georges-Edouard Cabriolet (1779–1848), whose name has for long been given, in vulgarly shortened form, to vehicles plying for passenger hire, and has recently been revived for motor-cars with folding tops. Again on an impulse, I reached for the dictionary that at the time I invariably carried with me. I looked up the word 'cabriolet'. There it was. I read the entry. I read it again. I could scarcely believe my eyes. No mention, no mention whatsoever, of the man whose very tomb I was that moment contemplating. Was there some sort of conspiracy?

It was there and then, standing in Père Lachaise cemetery, in a fine drizzle of rain as I remember, that I resolved to devote such time as I could spare to bringing overdue justice to Awning and Cabriolet and the rest, and to seeking out any others to whom the same injustice might have been done. By an odd, perhaps even an uncanny coincidence, when I was travelling back to London a few days later, I met in the bar of the boat-train an old acquaintance who, in the course of conversation, began to reminisce affectionately about the misfortunes of the impresario Alessandro Fiasco. My acquaintance, a great and knowledgeable lover of opera, knew about Fiasco. The Oxford English Dictionary, as I soon discovered, but no longer to my surprise, apparently did not. My resolve was hardened by this chance – if it *was* a chance – encounter.

This little book, as I have said, is the result of that resolve, and of a great deal of research and, I gladly and gratefully admit, perhaps an equally great amount of sheer serendipity. It is dedicated to the forgotten men and women whose brief lives I have tried to resurrect in its pages – or at least to the more agreeable and respectable of them, for, as was said of Matthew Doggerel's near-contemporary, Geoffrey Chaucer, 'all human life is there'. Worthy men and women or not, they have enriched our language. Did their ghosts – pining for recognition – guide my researches? I rather think they may have done so. *Has* there been some conspiracy to suppress their histories? Or was it simply that, though they left their names behind them, their lives were otherwise modest and obscure? I do not know. But I will end this Foreword with a word of warning to all compilers of English dictionaries. Whatever your motives may be, you have dismissed many of the men and women whose lives I have painstakingly reconstructed here with the words 'origin obscure'. Now you know better. I shall be scrutinizing future editions of your works in order to see whether the record has been corrected. If it has not I shall take whatever action is necessary. I shall call upon the ghosts of Goetz von Ransack and Jean Debris, or, if all else fails, that of Emily Satchel. You have been warned.

One final word. At the suggestion of another acquaintance of mine, a specialist in international copyright, in order to prevent idle lexicographers from simply incorporating my work wholesale I have included one name which *has* been recognized in standard dictionaries as eponymous. I shall not, for obvious reasons, reveal which it is.

JAMES COCHRANE
London, February 1992

Post scriptum

This book is of course the work of an amateur, albeit a devoted and enthusiastic one, and I cannot claim that it is definitive. I shall be glad to hear from readers, through my publishers, of other eponymous lives that I, as well as the dictionary mafia, have missed. I undertake that all well-authenticated entries will be incorporated in any future edition.

Von Asphalt on a bicycling tour
of his roads

AKIMBO, Mwawalele c.1780–?1813 Crown Prince of the West African state of Segu. During a prolonged visit to London in the early 1800s he was taken up by fashionable society, where his habit of standing with hands on hips and elbows out led to the term 'standing like Akimbo', later shortened to its present form. He returned to Segu on hearing of the illness of his father and disappeared, presumed killed, in a coup d'état, which brought to an end the Akimbo dynasty.

ASPHALT, Leopold von 1802–1880 German nobleman, born in Asphalt in Bavaria, who developed the roadmaking mixture of bitumen, pitch and sand to which his name is now commonly given. Having paved with it all the roads on his own considerable estates, he set out, with almost obsessive zeal, to pave as much as possible of Bavaria, where, it has been said, motor-car production was stimulated in order to find a use for Asphalt's roads. He was an early patron of Richard Wagner, who said of him, 'Asphalt is the only man in Germany who understands my sense of scale'. On the composer's vast productions Asphalt squandered that part of his fortune which was left over from road-making. He spent the last years of his life in Neuschwanstein Castle as a pensioner of King Ludwig II.

1

AVOCADO, Jorge-Luis de 1789–1868 Explorer and botanist, born in Buenos Aires, who made the tropical pear-shaped fruit familiar to European palates. Intrepid in the pursuit of unfamiliar vegetables and fruits, he visited every continent in the world, and was on the point of giving his name to the Kiwi fruit when he was reminded that he had already given it to the avocado. After his death, his mother, still alive at ninety-eight, was reported as saying, 'Jorge-Luis was always in a hurry. If only he'd waited, he could have given his name to something nice, like Baked Alaska'.

'intrepid in the pursuit
of unfamiliar vegetables'

AWNING, Edward 1826–1900 English sailor.
During a cruise in the Indian Ocean in 1853,
when he was serving as flag lieutenant to Rear-
Admiral Brindsley, the flagship docked at
Trincomalee and a party of ladies and gentlemen
came aboard for a luncheon. When it became
evident that the heat, whether in the admiral's
stateroom or on deck, would be insufferable for
the ladies, Lieutenant Awning, with great
resourcefulness, caused the bosun's work-party to
rig a canvas shelter over the quarterdeck, to the
great relief of all. This innovation spread rapidly
through the fleet and was later adopted for
civilian use. Awning's career was otherwise
undistinguished. A report on him by a senior
officer when he was seeking promotion stated that
'Unfortunately his willingness to please is not
matched by his professional competence.'

BIGOT, Nathaniel 1575–1660 Puritan preacher
and activist, born in Ipswich of Huguenot stock.
From his early youth he displayed signs of that
obstinate and intolerant zeal which was to
characterize his life. Coming to London in the
1590s, he was frequently ejected from the Globe
theatre for preaching loudly against vanity during
the quieter moments of Shakespeare's plays. An
early adherent of the Puritan movement, he failed
to obtain membership of any of its sects, which
found his views too extreme. He spent the Civil
War years preaching behind the Parliamentarian

lines until arrested as a nuisance by Cromwell. He condemned the young John Bunyan as frivolous, and was loud in his calls for the execution of King Charles I. It is likely that he would have been executed himself at the Restoration if he had not died of an apoplexy at the sight of Charles II returning to London.

BINGE, Sir Oswald 1678–1768 English country squire, born on his ancestral estate in Leicestershire, who became notable for the scale and duration of his eating and drinking bouts. In one recorded dinner at his club in London he is said to have consumed, with three friends, two dozen venison pasties, an entire roast pig, twenty quails, four brace each of partridge, pheasant and grouse, a dozen bottles of claret and five of port. His entertainments were said to be even more spacious at his home in Leicestershire, where a feast might last for several days, the guests coming and going while Sir Oswald remained at the table, taking occasional cat-naps. He was satirized in the *Tatler* by Addison and Steele, and castigated by his doctors, most of whom he outlived.

Sir Oswald (second from right) enjoying a light supper

'success did not come quickly'

BOATER, Charles Edwin 1838–1903 Hatmaker, born in Whitechapel, London. In the early 1860s he introduced the flat-crowned straw hat, inspired by seamen's headgear, that bears his name. Success did not come quickly, mainly because Boater started his sales campaign among the deeply conservative London working class. But once the style had been taken up by young public schoolboys it rapidly established itself, enjoying a vogue that lasted until the 1920s and is still revived from time to time.

BOGUS, Harold, aka Charles Edward Stewart, aka George Bonaparte, aka Maximilian Sneed, etc. c.1790–?   It is not known where or when Harold Bogus was born, or indeed whether that was his real name. He is first recorded on Mississippi river-boats in the 1820s, offering for sale (and more than once selling) a machine for converting cabbage leaves into bank-notes. Frequently arrested, he rarely spent more than a few hours in gaol, having bought his

Harold Bogus: a rare portrait (it is not clear what he is doing with his hat)

way out with a bundle of what proved to be counterfeit bills. In later years, when even the gullible became wary of Bogus machines and Bogus notes, he changed his name and his business methods, at one time selling the Mexican National Debt to a group of bankers in Charleston. He was last sighted in 1862, posing as Papal Nuncio to the government of the Confederacy under the name of Balthazar de Castiglione, and it is not known what role he may have played in history after that date.

BOLLARD, Frederick 1798–1876   English sailor, born in Portsmouth. After an unremarkable career, he was serving there as a captain on half pay when he began to notice how much damage was done to ships by the then practice of tying up to any convenient object on the quayside. In 1842 he began a campaign of letter-writing to the Admiralty and the Press which resulted in an Act of Parliament of 1844 requiring the provision of wooden, or preferably iron posts at fixed intervals in all Her Majesty's Naval Dockyards and ordering that all Her Majesty's ships should thenceforth be secured to these and not to 'trees, coal-merchants' carts or willing urchins, as heretofore'. Three years later the Navy Board noted that the cost of repairs had gone down by 17%. Captain Bollard was voted a pension of £140 per annum and retired soon after to the Isle of Wight, where he spent the remainder of a blameless and uneventful life.

BOTCH, Jeremy c.1770–1834 English jobbing carpenter and brick-layer, notorious for the unreliable character of his work. He was employed briefly on the construction of Brighton Pavilion – where the phrase 'a Botch job' first became current – but was dismissed when a chinois screen he had made fell on the heads of the Prince Regent and Mrs Fitzherbert. He spent the rest of his life wandering around the British Isles in search of places his reputation had not yet reached. It has been suggested, convincingly, that the phrase 'jerry-built' may also derive from his name and reputation.

'in search of places his reputation had not reached'

9

BOUDOIR, Emmeline 1863–1937   Born
Emmeline Leboeuf to a humble peasant family in
the Perigord region of France and a remarkable
beauty, she went to Paris while in her teens,
married the financier Georges Boudoir, thirty
years older than herself, and became a leading
figure in the Parisian demi-monde. Her custom of
entertaining friends, both male and female, in a
small, charmingly decorated private sitting-room
was the cause of her giving her name to the
French, and later the English, language. It was
said that even in the last year of her life she
received as many as forty male admirers,
including Marshal Petain, Maurice Chevalier and
Jean-Paul Sartre.

Emmeline Boudoir (right)
relaxes with a friend

BUFFET, Pierre-Alphonse 1692–1756 French gentleman-gambler, born in Paris, who introduced the custom of having food laid on a side-board for guests to serve themselves as and when they wished. In one version of his story he was obliged to sell his dinner table during a run of bad luck, in another he simply gave it away after deciding that time spent eating at a table was time denied to his beloved cards. Whatever the explanation, 'Buffet suppers' became the rage among loose-living people in his native Paris, and soon after in London and elsewhere. His house in the Place des Vosges, which he rarely left, became a refuge for Parisians weary of 'Enlightenment' conversation. It was said that nothing was ever heard there but the soft flutter of playing cards, the murmuring of bets, and the occasional oath.

BUGLE, Hereward 1880–1934 A former military bandsman, who served with Baden-Powell at the

'it was said that he could play almost anything'

siege of Mafeking, he developed the instrument that bears his name in his spare time while working as a chartered surveyor in Birmingham. In later life he was much involved, as instrumentalist, conductor and even composer (*Solihull Serenade*, 1921, *Minuet for Brass*, 1925), in the burgeoning brass band movement in the Midlands and North of England, but it was his greatest achievement to be appointed, in 1911, Musical Director to Baden Powell's recently formed Boy Scout Movement. A considerable virtuoso on all wind instruments, it was said that he could play almost anything. He died, prematurely, of a prolapsed embouchure.

CABARET, Antoine de 1749–93   Born in Perigueux, Cabaret came to Paris in 1775. In 1778 he opened a café in the Rue du Bac, where he introduced the practice

Cabaret shortly before his death

of entertaining customers in the evening with songs and comedy turns. Originally named simply Antoine Cabaret, after his success he awarded himself the aristocratic particle, a piece of snobbery that may well have cost him his life, since he was sent to the guillotine in the Great Terror, after being denounced as an aristocrat and frivolous parasite.

CABRIOLET, Georges-Edouard 1779–1848 French equestrian. After a riding accident in 1816 left him with injuries which prevented him from sitting a horse with any comfort, he designed and had built for him a light, one-horse, two-wheeled chaise, whose bounding motion was the closest he could achieve to the sensation of bestriding a thoroughbred. His design, built for him by English carriage-makers, was soon copied by young bloods in London and Paris (and later by the owners of coaches plying for hire), but Cabriolet himself lived out the remainder of his life in a constant state of frustration. His attempts to follow the hounds in his carriage resulted in several further injuries, and he died while charging the Paris mob in it in the Revolution of 1848.

CAMI, Vittorio 1859–1914 Italian couturier, born in Turin. He opened his first salon in Milan in 1883 and moved to Paris in 1886. His clothes, made on voluptuous lines and employing

'constantly on the look-out for new models'

expensive fabrics, enjoyed a brief vogue, but he is nowadays remembered only for the one-piece female undergarment he invented. Increasingly interested in lingerie in his middle years, he was constantly on the look-out for new models. He committed suicide in August 1914.

CARBURETTO, Emilio 1845–1917   The
famous Italian inventor was born in Spoleto and
studied at the University of Bologna. Trained as
an engineer, he was one of the founding members
of the Touring Club of Italy, which awarded him
its Supreme Grand Cross in 1900 for his
'inestimable contribution to the development of
the motor car'. A reserve officer in the Bersaglieri,
he was killed while directing ambulance services
at the battle of Caporetto.

*'his inestimable
contribution'*

CAROUSEL, Leonid 1790–1845   Equestrian, showman and inventor of mixed Russian and French parentage, born in Paris where his father was in the Imperial Russian consular service. He himself volunteered for service in one of Napoleon's hussar regiments during the Emperor's last Hundred Days, after which he emigrated to

the United States. There he briefly studied engineering before joining a travelling show as equestrian acrobat and mechanic. The first example of his steam-driven merry-go-round appeared in Wyoming in 1843. He died after being trampled by a circus elephant in Des Moines, Iowa.

Leonid Carousel (left) in his youth, and (right) shortly before his death

CARTEL, Edmond 1822–1891 and Georges 1825–1900 French financiers, born in Rennes. Having made a fortune in grain speculation in the 1850s they moved to Paris and began the practice of encouraging firms to combine in order to maintain prices which bears their unsavoury name.

Edmond (left) *and Georges Cartel in London at the height of their career*

Finding the Paris Bourse too restrictive they transferred their activities to New York and Chicago, where they quadrupled their capital, dealing mainly in pork futures and railroad stocks. Legislation in the 1870s clipped their wings somewhat, and they ended their days as pig-breeders in Alsace.

CHASSIS, Benoit de 1827–1899 This important pioneer in the history of motoring was born into a family of wealthy landowners near Aix-en-Provence, and, given the fundamental nature of his contribution, it is remarkable that he was almost entirely self-taught, claiming that he

*'a combined milk-float and
passenger service'*

*Matthew Coffin at work on one of his more
elaborate models*

was educated by the local blacksmith. Enthusiasm for all aspects of early motoring dissipated his inheritance. An attempt to recoup his fortune by setting up a combined milk-float and passenger service merely left him deeper in debt, and he would have been bankrupted had he not ended his life in a fatal crash while racing at Deauville.

COFFIN, Matthew c.1480–1540 English carpenter, born in London. He developed the wooden 'Coffin box' while working for the monks of Blackfriars, and when they rejected it on theological grounds, preferring the traditional stone article, he went into business on his own account and did a lively trade among the tradesmen of Southwark and the City. It is interesting that in a transitional period of English art and design he offered his customers the choice of 'Gothic' or 'Italian' styles. He was Lord Mayor of London 1531–33.

COMMA, Domenico da 1264–1316 The inventor of one of our most familiar marks of punctuation was born in Mantua and entered the Dominican order sometime before 1300, devoting the remainder of his life to scholarship. A near-contemporary of Dante, who travelled extensively among the universities and monasteries of the Europe of his time, arguing for the usefulness of his little mark, he was at one point arraigned before the Inquisition on charges of heresy, on the grounds that no such punctuation was to be found in the scriptures, in the Early Church Fathers or even in classical literature, but he seems to have survived the experience unscathed.

Comma arguing his case at
the University of Paris

CORSET, Etienne c.1760–1832 French military
tailor, born in Strasbourg, who learned his trade
making uniforms for the armies of Frederick the
Great of Prussia but later moved to Paris. The
boned and stiffened undergarments he designed
and made helped to preserve the figures of French
officers after they had passed their first youth. He
was imprisoned as a Royalist lackey during the
French Revolution, but survived to equip the
officers of Napoleon's splendid cavalry and their
successors after the Bourbon restoration. His
designs were later adapted by others for women's
use.

Etienne Corset in prison

CULVERT, Sir Roderick 1801–1882 Civil
engineer, born in Manchester and largely self-
educated. He early specialized in canal construction, and his experience in passing water under
roads and tramways served him well when he
threw himself into the problems created by the
rapid expansion of railways in the 1840s. His
work, both in Britain and the United States, was
well-designed, but often suffered from hasty
execution and poor materials. He was knighted in
1865.

'hasty execution and poor materials'

CURRY, Sir George 1826–1890 British soldier, born in Berwick-on-Tweed. He spent his entire career in the service of the East India Company and later of the Indian Army and rose to the rank of general. He was the first officer of the British Raj to develop a taste for the highly spiced stews of the natives, and in consequence dined alone for many years. His attempt to introduce mutton

'in consequence dined alone'

vindaloo and chapatis into the mess of his own British Tommies resulted in one of the lesser known mutinies of the period. It was only after Queen Victoria was seen eating some of it at a luncheon for visiting rajahs in 1869 that the habit of eating the food that had become known as 'Curry' began to spread among the British community in general.

DEBRIS, Jean 1325–1369 Gascon mercenary soldier, who fought mainly on the English side in the Hundred Years War, thought to have been born in Bayonne. Even in a period of unusual savagery he gained a reputation for utter ruthlessness, especially in his treatment of towns the forces under his command captured after a siege, when, as Froissart put it, 'it was a matter of pride with him to leave no stone standing upon another'. His name entered the language due to a misunderstanding. Coming upon the ruins of a town he had recently visited, an English knight pointed to the piles of rubble and enquired of his French companion what on earth it was. The Frenchman shrugged and replied, 'C'est Debris.' When the tide of war turned, Debris briefly transferred his services to the French, but died in a brawl over pay in a Paris tavern.

DENIM, Oscar 1838–1899 Born in Linz, he emigrated to New York in 1862 and spent the remainder of his life in the American West, peddling the hard-wearing blue cloth to which he gave his name. Although his attempts to export the fabric were largely unsuccessful he made a considerable fortune. He devoted the last years of his life to many charitable causes, including the foundation of the Denim Travelling Scholarships, which provided clothing and money to young Americans travelling in Europe and elsewhere. His autobiography, *My Blue Heaven* (Scribners), was published posthumously in 1901.

*'his attempts to export the fabric were
largely unsuccessful'*

DERRICK, c.1565–1630 Public hangman,
known only by that name, who was performing
his duties at Tyburn in the early 1600s. Nothing is
known of his life, save that he might have been of
Dutch ancestry, but he did his dreadful work
either for so long or so strikingly well that he
became identified with it in the public mind. It
was probably sailors, with their love of gallows
humour, who first gave his name to the crane-like
contrivance used on board ships for lifting and
moving weights, and to similar machines on land.

27

DIAPER, Horace 1857–1922
Born in Minneapolis, he was
obliged to drop out of medical
studies at Harvard in order to
run the family drapery business
after the death of his father.
It was there that, starting
from first principles, he
used his scientific and
medical knowledge to
develop the hygienic
infants' napkins that
have been such a
boon and a blessing
to mankind through-
out the civilized
world. His consider-
able fortune was
devoted to research
and development
in the area of
family planning.

'starting from first principles'

DOGGEREL or **DOGGREL**, Matthew
c.1330–1405 Medieval English poet, born, it is
thought, in Oxford, whose work would have been
entirely forgotten had he not been briefly mentioned by Geoffrey Chaucer, who is known to have

borrowed and improved upon some of his verses.
He was a member of the guild of candlemakers,
and may well have contributed to some of the
Mystery plays of the time. Only fragments of his
work survive, of which 'Whan that Aprille with his
shoures wet/Hath caused us all to mourne and fret'
is all-too-typical.

DOLDRUM, Frederick 1784–1839 English sailor.
Though he rose to the rank of post-captain in the
Royal Navy, his career was beset by misfortune,
chiefly in the form of those long spells of windless
calm to which he gave his name. He served almost
exclusively on detached duty and arrived late at the
battle of Trafalgar. Ironically, he died when his ship
went down in a typhoon in the Azores.

Frederick Doldrum: the last sighting

DUDGEON, Miles 1541–1604 A one-time
soldier, who later became an actor in the Lord
Chamberlain's company, he was proverbial in
both professions for his readiness to take offence
and to fly into a rage over apparently trifling
matters. There is a legend that Shakespeare knew

Miles Dudgeon

him from the days when they both served in the
Low Countries and based several of his characters
on him, including Pistol in *Henry IV* and *Henry V*,
but dared not use his name for fear of violent
retaliation.

DUFFEL, George Henry 1796–1843 Born,
probably, in Chatham, he served as a purser in the
Navy from 1795 to 1822. Suffering, as most

pursers did, from complaints about the quality of the 'slops' he sold to the seamen as clothing, he bought a quantity of woollen cloth in Rotterdam that had been rejected by the citizens there as too heavy and coarse. Sewn into simple coats, it was greatly appreciated by sailors on watch in wintry seas, and Duffel enjoyed both profit and popularity for the remainder of his career, though he did not live to see his coats worn by officers and gentlemen.

Matthias Easel at work

EASEL, Matthias c.1410–1470 The man whose humble invention transformed the face of art in the western world was born in Nuremberg and apprenticed to a muralist there. An indifferent painter himself, he seems to have had a gift for

Fiasco receives news of yet another disaster

carpentry which led him to develop his revolu-
tionary device. This was at first condemned by the
Church, which correctly foresaw that it would
lead to the production of profane imagery, but it
was taken up with enthusiasm by the artists of the
time. No painting of his own survives, though a
Bowl of Fruit with Wineglass in the Rijksmuseum
in Amsterdam is tentatively attributed to his
studio.

FIASCO, Alessandro 1792–1869 Italian opera
director and impresario, born in Trieste, who
became legendary for the disasters that attended
many of his productions. In his *Barber of Seville*
at Verona in 1823 the barber almost severed the
ear of the soprano; in *Lucia di Lammermoor* at
Mantua in 1837 the stage collapsed during a
Highland dance, injuring several of the
performers; and in his *Norma* at Padua in 1839 a
large moon made of pewter fell from the flies and
nearly decapitated one of the leading tenors of the
day. Whether these accidents were the result of
bad luck or ill judgement never became clear, but
Fiasco was obliged to leave Italy for England,
where misfortune continued to dog his career. He
was though instrumental in heightening London's
awareness of Rossini, Donizetti and Bellini.

FIRKIN, Matthew 1620–1683 English brewer
and tavern-keeper, born in Deptford, who had
made for him the barrels of moderate size that

bear his name, so that customers might conveniently carry home for their own use quantities of his renowned ale. Samuel Pepys mentions him in his diary for 4 October, 1664: 'Supped with Sir W[illiam] Batten and Mr. Coventry at the Ostrich in Cheapside, and so liked Mr. Firkin's ale there that we had one of his excellent small barrels of it brought with us to my house, and were very merry, until Sir W. offended my dear Wife, by goosing her, but we did not much care, being un-common merry. And so to bed.' (The Firkin barrel contained nine gallons).

'uncommon merry'

FURLONG, Giles c.1280–1347 Wealthy English peasant, whose interminable boundary disputes led to the first rational system of land measurement since Roman times. Geoffrey Chaucer's father, a wine merchant, lost a large part of the land he had bought in Suffolk to the wily Furlong (without whose dealings, it must be admitted, the Father of English Poetry might have been a landowner rather than an author) and the poet Doggerel (q.v.) wrote of him: 'Were ich neghbor to Giles Furlong/Ich coud not stond that cur long.' An inveterate litigant, he died, unmourned by his neighbours, in the Black Death.

Giles Furlong sharpening his scythe

FURLOUGH, George c.1600–1686 English private soldier, born near Taunton in Somerset, who joined the army at the age of sixteen and fought for the Royalist cause in the Civil War. A simple country lad, he was apt to leave his duties and return home to visit his mother whenever the impulse took him. Whether because of the sheer amiability of his character, or because he served under kindly captains, this proclivity of his seems to have been regarded as more endearing than felonious. Though he was never promoted, neither was he ever severely punished. The jocular expression 'to grant a Furlough' for compassionate leave soon entered army parlance, and Furlough himself became one of the first pensioners at the Royal Hospital, Chelsea.

GADGET, Walter 1848–1918 Born in Harrisburg, Pennsylvania, where he also lived and died, Walter Gadget joined the now long-

Walter Gadget demonstrates the Patent Foolproof Pancake Tosser defunct department store (and later mail order company) of Lewison-Murphy at the age of sixteen. A hard-working young man, of no particular talent, he rose slowly but steadily in the company until at the age of twenty-nine he was made buyer-in-charge of the department selling small ingenious domestic tools and devices, which American inventiveness was proliferating at that time. Since there was no known collective name for such merchandise it became known as Gadget's, thus earning ever-lasting fame for this honest toiler in the vineyards. Gadget remained at his post until his honourable retirement in 1908. He was an early and much-respected member of Rotary, and had two sons, both of whom became successful lawyers.

GALOSH, Joseph 1839–1909
The inventor of the rubber overshoe was born in Manchester to a family of Hungarian descent, which however emigrated to the USA in 1849. Although it bears his name,

'other ventures … were unsuccessful'

he did not succeed in patenting his invention, which was rapidly imitated by several manufacturers. Other ventures of his were unsuccessful, and he died in poverty.

GASKET, Alfred 1842–1913 Born in Plattsville, Pennsylvania, Gasket was a self-taught mechanic. After service in the Union artillery in the Civil War, he drifted into the railroad business, developing in his spare time the simple but vital device that revolutionized engineering and made possible the automotive industry. A simple, modest man, he took out no patents and died in poverty and obscurity.

Alfred Gasket: the quiet genius

GINGHAM, Martha c.1580–1648 English bawdy-house keeper. Her brothel, in the London Borough of Southwark, specialized in young, fresh-looking country girls, whom Mistress Gingham dressed, at her own expense, in clean petticoats and neat frocks of a striped or chequered pattern, made from cloth supplied to her by friendly sailors. She married respectably in 1622 and moved to Richmond, where she opened a chop-house of impeccable reputation that later became a tea-shop.

GUSSET, Florence 1779–1845 English seam-stress, born in Islington. Her skill with the needle soon brought her a wealthy and fashion-able clientele, but she owes her place in history to her invention of a simple,

'low, "fast", or foreign women'

comfortable and above all, decorous insertion of fabric joining the legs of ladies' drawers or pantaloons, which made such garments acceptable in respectable English society. They had previously been worn only by low, 'fast', or foreign women. In 1839 she became drawer-maker by Royal Warrant to the young Queen Victoria.

HABERDASHER, Richard c.1500–1567 English merchant, born in Saffron Walden, Essex. Of obscure parentage, he came to London in c.1520 as a peddlar of miscellaneous small dress accessories, ribbons, trimmings, etc. Unusually successful in this line, he had first a regular stall at St Bartholomew's Fair and then a permanent shop in St Aldgate's in the City of London, where persons both high and low came to buy his wares. Because of the oddity of his name (probably of North German origin) he was interrogated as a possible spy by agents of Sir Francis Walsingham, but satisfied them of his innocence, though he never quite recovered his health.

HAMMOCK, William c.1530–1589 English seaman, who earned the gratitude of sailors the world over for his invention of the slung canvas bed (which in all probability he borrowed from the Carib Indians he encountered on his voyages with Sir Francis Drake). For men used to sleeping

Haberdasher in the early years

on the wet, cold and often filthy decks of the ships of the time, Hammock's innovation was seen as a godsend. He was born in Plymouth and served as a seaman from the age of twelve until his death. An amiable, idle man, he was present, as a carpenter's mate, at the engagement with the Spanish Armada in 1588, but is thought to have slept through most of it.

HAVERSACK, Emil 1819–1888 Born in Strasbourg, he spent his entire life in the French (later the Imperial German) postal service. His humble device for easing his burden by carrying it

'An early version'

on his back was widely imitated, and spread by postmen throughout the western world. An early version is shown in the illustration.

HOARDING, Sir Samuel 1820–1901 The man who first erected screens for public advertisement sprang from obscurity in the East End of London.

Sir Samuel Hoarding directs the placing of an advertisement

Seeing the opportunities offered by the new railways, he rented sites along the lines for a few shillings and sold space to the advertisers of patent medicines. He made a vast fortune while still in his thirties, and devoted the rest of his life to good works. He was knighted in 1867.

*Hoist receives medical attention after
an accident with explosives*

HOIST, Samuel c.1535–1599 English pioneer-
sergeant, who fought mainly in the Low Countries
and there developed tackle for lifting and moving
siege equipment, including the heavy mines
known as petards which were used to breach
walls. Hoist's devices were not regarded as
particularly reliable by his fellow-pioneers, who
tended to keep out of the way when he was
handling explosives. The cry, 'There goes Hoist
with his own petard' was often heard around the

English siege-lines, and before long entered the language, though few understood what it meant.

HOLSTER, Sir Edmund 1642–1709 English gentleman and soldier. As an officer in the Coldstream Guards he had the good fortune to serve during a relatively peaceful time in English history, but on more than one occasion, whether through insobriety or natural clumsiness, narrowly missed injuring himself severely through his habit of carrying loaded pistols in the pockets of his military coat. When one such accident had come close to destroying his manhood he went to his boot-maker and commanded him to make a pair of stout leather cases that could be fitted to his saddle or to his own belt. Thereafter he suffered only slight bruises, and his brother-officers, who had themselves suffered similarly more often than they were prepared to admit, quietly copied his innovation.

HUMDINGER, Arnold 1897–1932 American aviator, born in Philadelphia and educated at Andover and Yale, where he excelled in track and field events as well as academically, graduating *maxima cum laude* in 1921. Strikingly handsome, a brilliant raconteur and wit, an outstanding tennis player, a chess-master and a virtuoso pianist in the manner of both Rachmaninov and Cole Porter, he was the most eligible bachelor of his day, and was frequently offered starring roles in Hollywood. He chose instead, however, to serve his country by joining the US Army Air Corps, in which he rose to the rank of lieutenant-colonel at the age of twenty-eight, on several occasions just failing to win the Schneider Trophy in experimental air-planes he had designed himself. His tragically early death, during an attempt to land his single-seater Curtiss biplane on the summit of Mt Everest, was overshadowed by the Lindbergh kidnapping in the same year, but he remained a hero and a legend to young American pilots, who gave his name to exceptionally fast air-planes and automobiles, and to anything that was excellent in its class.

KETCHUP, Noah c.1680–1746 Born in what is now Ohio, and almost certainly of Huron Indian descent, he arrived in Philadelphia c.1700. There, after working unsuccessfully at a variety of occupations, as a last resort he began bottling and selling the excellent tomato and mushroom relishes that his wife, Martha, had for long put up for use in the home. Ketchup sauces soon entered the cuisine of the American Colonies and before long were put into large scale commercial production, though Ketchup himself never earned more than a modest living.

Martha Ketchup (left) *prepares her famous relish, and Noah samples the product*

KIOSK, Imre 1862–1921 Born in Budapest, the
son of an innkeeper, Kiosk, while still a young
man, made a vast fortune with a chain of tiny
shops or stalls selling tobacco, newspapers, soft
drinks and lottery tickets. Before the First World
War there were over four hundred such shops
throughout the Austro-Hungarian Empire.

*Imre Kiosk inspects
his wares*

Politically of the extreme right, Kiosk was an
early supporter of the nationalist factions which
later grew into the National Socialist Party.
Ruined by the defeat of 1918, he died in poverty
in Vienna.

LACROSSE, Charles-Marie 1779–1842 Born in
Trois Rivières, Quebec, he did not so much invent
as refine and codify the rules of the game that
bears his name, which is of American Indian

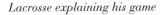

Lacrosse explaining his game

origin. Encountering resistance to his attempts to introduce it into schools, he travelled the length and breadth of the country, explaining its merits to trappers, hunters and voyageurs. In his version there were up to 1000 players on each side, the goals were three miles apart and the ball was made of deerskin. The game did not really take off among Europeans until the rules were modified, shortly after his death.

LAGER, Gottfried and Sigmund c.1400–1470 Founders of a notable family of German brewers. Their business was established in Dortmund, but sometime in the 1440s a violent quarrel over the accounts led to Gottfried's move to Munich, where the introduction of the brothers' pale, strong beer led to great prosperity. All the known descendents of both brothers were wiped out in the Thirty Years' War.

LAMBAST, Geoffrey 1588–1673 English schoolmaster, born in Shrewsbury. Educated at Oxford, where he was an undistinguished student and an amateur pugilist, he taught Mathematics and Divinity at a variety of schools including Westminster, Winchester and Eton, and became a notorious flogger. On his retirement in 1661 he obtained a curacy in Shropshire, where he was often heard to boast that he had 'reddened the a***s of half the gentlemen in England'.

Gottfried (left) *and Sigmund Lager at the moment of their quarrel, from a contemporary illustration*

LATRINE, Francois-Charles-Marie Deschamps, Marquis de 1744–1812 French aristocrat and soldier, who served in most of the wars of the eighteenth century. A stern disciplinarian, he was also devoted to the comfort and health of his men, whom he set to digging field privies whenever they ceased marching for more than a few minutes. He went into exile in Switzerland in 1790 but returned to France in 1799 to serve Napoleon as Inspector General of Field Hygiene. He died of gangrenous frostbite during the retreat from Moscow.

Latrine with his men

LOBBY, Sir Thomas c.1540–1601 A former scullion, he rose to become Clerk of Works to the household of Queen Elizabeth I. In that role he was confronted by the problem that in the residences for which he was responsible all the sleeping chambers led directly from one to another, so that it was impossible to reach any

room without passing through all the rooms
preceding it. This led to many inconveniences, not
the least of which was the difficulty of conducting
assignations with any degree of discretion. As
manners grew more polite in the course of the
century, this situation was increasingly found to
be intolerable. Thomas Lobby did much to

alleviate the problem by taking every opportunity
– whether in building new palaces or renovating
old ones – to have constructed a passage or
corridor which allowed independent access to
sleeping rooms. (The considerable cost of this was
off-set by selling three of the remaining English
monasteries.) It is hard to over-estimate the social
consequences of Lobby's innovation, which was
before long copied in the larger private houses

A gentleman of the court discreetly rewards
Thomas Lobby for his services

throughout the country. He was knighted in 1582 and received many substantial purses from gentlemen and ladies of the court.

MANGLE, Herbert 1811–1882 The inventor of what was to be a great boon to the nineteenth century housewife and domestic servant was born

'Less cumbersome models followed'

in Manchester, where he also trained as an engineer. It was his ambition to improve the efficiency of the steam locomotive, but pressure from his wife led him to construct the prototype of what became the Mangle Patent Linen-smoother and Laundry-aid. Less cumbersome models followed, but not before Mangle's wife had died of a heart-attack following over-exertion, and he returned to locomotive design, in which he played a modest part in the closing decades of the century.

MARMELADO, Joao c.1450–1510
Portuguese inn-keeper, born in Lisbon. Receiving there a large consignment of Seville oranges in payment of a debt, and recognizing that he could not use them in the normal course of things before they became well-rotted, he instructed his servants to boil them in a large vat with sugar. He found the resulting confection unpalatable, but nonetheless had dishes of it placed on the tables for his guests to take or not as they pleased. The guests, having tried it once with grilled sardines or roast chicken, tended to push it to one side, and Marmelado was on the point of consigning the whole boiling to the pigs when a party of English merchants arrived. They did not touch the sticky orange substance at their evening meal, but the following morning, with increasingly loud murmurs of approval, they began to spread it upon toasted bread, and thus consume it. The rest

is history. On the day of their departure the
merchants took with them three hundredweight
of Marmelado's concoction, after many toasts to
the oldest alliance.

MARZIPAN, Maria-Theresa, Marquise de
c.1760–1827   Born in Stepney, London, as Eliza
Marchpane, this famous courtesan travelled, at the
expense of her various lovers, throughout Europe.
She took the (entirely invented) title of Marquise
de Marzipan while living as the mistress of Prince
Mwawalele Akimbo (q.v.) in London in 1801.
Earlier she had almost certainly seduced the
young Wolfgang Amadeus Mozart in Vienna,
where she discovered her passion for sweetmeats
made of sugar and crushed almonds. Her devotion
to this confection, which she introduced into
England, led to her becoming immensely stout, a
fact which did not prevent her becoming the
mistress of the Prince Regent and the subject of a
cartoon by Rowlandson. She died, peacefully, in
Brighton.

MASCOT, Jacques c.1400–1443   Beloved
dwarf at the court of Philip the Good, Duke of
Burgundy. Only just over three feet in height when
fully grown, he was known for the quickness of his
wit and the sweetness of his disposition. He was
adopted by the Duke, whom he advised on affairs
of state, and was reputed to have had many illicit
affairs with ladies of the court, though without, it

Mascot joins the Duke for a wine and cheese lunch

seems, ever causing offence. After his death, which was greatly mourned, the Duke, in memory of him, gave his name to a pet spaniel of his, and to a tame goose, of which he was very fond.

MORGUE, Jules 1799–1874 French business-man, born in Paris, where he also served in the National Guard. Finding himself penniless after some rash speculation, and having exhausted

58

every other means of recovering his fortune, he at last had the idea of offering his house for rent to the Paris police as a place where corpses might be laid out while they awaited identification. The Paris police readily took up the offer, and agreed further to keep him regularly supplied with quantities of ice, at their expense, in the months

Morgue explains his plan to Mme Morgue

*Lorenzo Motto timing himself while writing
forty poems per hour*

between April and September. The house was
rapidly filled, including the bedroom used by
Morgue and his wife, in which, he claimed, they
slept like the dead.

MOTTO, Lorenzo 1382–1459 Italian minor
poet, born in Siena. Writing in both Latin and
Italian, in his youth he attempted works on an
epic scale, including a verse *History of the World*
in 600 cantos. Unable to find a patron for this, he
transferred his talents to religious and amatory
sonnets in the manner of Petrarch. When these
also failed to win recognition he began to produce
shorter and shorter works until, in his early 40s,
he began to achieve considerable success with
one- or two-line verses, which he had copied onto
cards and sold to accompany gifts or to convey
greetings. When he had the idea of producing
these in Latin for the coats-of-arms of newly
ennobled bourgeois, his fortune was made. He
himself became a *marchese* in 1449 and took the
'Motto' *Brevis Dulcisque*.

MOUSTACHE, Geoffroy de Cissac, Sieur de
1529–1590 French nobleman and soldier, born
on his family estate near Bordeaux. He was
probably not the first young man of the time to
sport the new fashion of shaving the cheeks and
chin while allowing the hair on the upper lip to
grow, but his own swaggering temperament
identified him with it in the popular mind. By the

61

1580s, any young gentle-
man wearing his facial
hair in that way was
likely to be pursued
by urchins shouting
'M'sieur Moustache,
M'sieur Moustache!'
Nevertheless the
fashion survived,
and was before
long taken up
by the English
and readily
assimilated
along with
the wine of
the region.

Moustache:
the only known
portrait

NATTY, George William 1871–1933 Baseball player, born in Poughkeepsie, NY. Batting for the Yankees, he had several successful seasons in the 1890s, but a certain excessive neatness in his dress tended to elicit mockery from low elements in the crowd and he was dropped in 1897 and never played again. He ran for governor in 1903 under the slogan 'Natty can do it', but otherwise spent the rest of his life in obscurity.

'a certain excessive neatness'

NIBLICK, Horace 1817–1898   English
amateur golfer, born in Liverpool. An ironmonger
by trade, he took up the game in middle-age.

Horace Niblick ponders a putt

Frustrated, while playing at Hoylake, by his
inability to play the ball out of ruts and whin
bushes with the existing clubs, he spent two years
designing a club of his own, which he introduced
in 1862. This rapidly won acceptance throughout
the golfing world, though Niblick himself never
succeeded in breaking ninety.

NUGGET, George Alfred 1817–1882   Born in Oldham, George Alfred Nugget drifted from job to job until in 1848 he received news of the California Gold Rush. Spending his savings on the cost of passage, he made his way to Sutter's Mill and there bought a small claim. Within a few months he had distinguished himself by the frequency with which he would rush to the banks with lumps of rock or compacted clay, claiming that they contained traces of the precious metal. Eventually, quite penniless and a hopeless alcoholic, he took on employment as a bottle-washer in an hotel, where his maudlin reminiscences about the gold he had almost found became proverbial.

PARQUET, Jean-Phillipe 1638–?1680   French carpenter, born in Versailles in the same year as his master, Louis XIV. His work was patronized by Cardinal Mazarin, and he was employed to lay the floors at the great new palace of the young king, who admired his neat

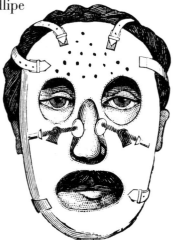

Probably not the 'Man in the Iron Mask'

'constantly in pursuit of larger game'

method of laying short planks in a manner reminiscent of Flemish brick-laying. Unfortunately for him, he was discovered eavesdropping a conversation between the king and Madame de Montespan, and was imprisoned under *lettres de cachet* and never heard of again. It has been suggested, unconvincingly, that he was the famous 'Man in the Iron Mask'.

PILCHARD, Matthew c.1780–1842   English fisherman, born in St Ives, Cornwall. This unfortunate man, though constantly in pursuit of larger game, found himself unable to catch anything in quantity except the small sardine-like fish which his fellow fishermen so despised that they commonly threw them back into the sea and never troubled to give them a name. In desperation, Pilchard was reduced to offering these in the market for sale to the poorest classes of people, and thus eked out a precarious living until the virtues of the tiny fish – when grilled, and served on warm toast – became more widely recognized.

PILLORY, Sir Matthew c.1560–1632   English magistrate, born on his family estate near Devizes in Wiltshire. A compassionate man, of reforming temperament, on becoming a magistrate in 1528 he began the practice of commuting the death sentence for crimes involving goods of value less than ten pence. So that offenders should nonetheless not go unpunished, nor the town gaol be overcrowded, he devised and had built the structure that bears his name. Felons were confined in it for a number of hours or days according to the severity of the offence and subjected to public ridicule and pelting with objects either hard or soft, depending on their popularity with the town mob. The device was before long adopted throughout the country and remained in use until it was abolished in 1837.

POCKET, Henry 1589–1645   English gentleman, born in Richmond, Surrey, who was the first to have the idea of having his breeches made with a small internal purse or pouch, access to which was gained through a slit in the sides. His contemporaries, who carried their money and other small possessions in a purse slung from the belt, treated this innovation with derision at first, accusing him of keeping coins in his codpiece and making other similar merry jests at his expense. However, the practice gradually caught on, especially when it was perceived that it was also a convenient means of keeping the hands warm in winter.

POLTROON, Sir Walter 1538–1611   Anglo-Flemish knight, born in Ghent, noted for his craven cowardice. Though he devoted a large fortune, derived from the wool trade, to the accoutrements of knighthood, he went to considerable pains to avoid dangerous service in the wars of the time, and did most of his fighting in tournaments, in which, it was said, no trick was too low for him to stoop to. He has been suggested as a model for Shakespeare's Falstaff, but seems to have lacked all the latter's saving graces.

'no trick was too low'

RANSACK, Goetz von 1598–1649   Soldier-of-fortune of mixed German and Danish ancestry, born in Lübeck. He fought for several masters in the Thirty Years' War, having no particular religious convictions, and was notorious for his rapacity, which was remarkable even for those times. It was said of him that when a city fell to the troops under his command not even the rats

Von Ransack after a good day's work

were safe, everything of value being removed in
his baggage-train. He died – of a broken heart, it
was believed – not long after the Peace of
Westphalia.

RICOCHET, Marc-Antoine 1779–1846
French marksman, born in Rennes, noted for his
ability to hit a target indirectly by causing the

shot to rebound from a hard surface nearby. This skill, which called for an almost instinctive geometrical calculation, was of great value in house-to-house fighting during Napoleon's early campaigns, in which Ricochet served as a *voltigeur*. He is known to have been present as a marine sharp-shooter at the battle of Trafalgar, but it is unlikely that, as is sometimes suggested, he fired the shot that struck down Lord Nelson.

RINK, Jan-Willem van der 1689–1763   Born in Nijmegen, he is honoured among Netherlanders, and indeed among ice-skaters the world over, for his invention of the purposely frozen skating pond, which allowed more elaborate manoeuvres than the narrow canals of Holland, and whose value was increasingly recognized after the recession of the so-called Little Ice Age and the development of the modern steel skate-blade. He drowned, it is said, after demonstrating to friends the execution of a perfect ice-circle.

SALON, Henriette-Marie Destours, Marquise de 1680–1743   Born to a noble but impoverished family in Grenoble, she married the elderly and immensely rich Marquis de Salon in 1697. The marriage was one of convenience only. Having given the Marquis an heir in 1698, she led an independent life at her houses in Versailles and Paris, where the large apartments she had made for her entertainments were greatly admired and

The Marquise prepares for an evening at home

widely imitated. A woman of great wit and
beauty, she was wooed by Louis XIV and was for
a time the mistress of Louis XV.

SANDAL, Auguste 1840–1921   French
physician, born in Narbonne, Professor of
Medicine at the University of Toulouse 1879–

1908. In his early thirties he developed the conviction that constricting boots and shoes were deleterious to health and devoted the rest of his life to the design and promotion of comfortable and hygienic footware. In his later years he conducted an extensive correspondence with George Bernard Shaw and other members of the Fabian Society on vegetarianism, the evils of alcohol and tobacco, etc, etc. His magnum opus, *Le Pied*, was published in 1905.

Professor Sandal makes notes on unsuitable footwear

The Ladies' League of Self-Defence

SATCHEL, Emily 1834–1905   American poetess and early feminist, born in Boston. Though her poetry was admired by Henry James and her correspondence with the early English feminist movement has been preserved, she is now remembered chiefly for her contributions to the subject of what was then known as 'rational dress', in particular the simple and capacious purse or handbag that bears her name. She was the co-founder in 1883 of the Ladies' League of Self-Defence. She lived in Paris from 1890 until her death. Picasso painted her (*Femme avec sac à main*) and described her in one of his letters as 'cette femme insupportable'.

Emily Satchel in later life

SCAFFOLD, Sir Henry 1561–1634   English judge, born in Durham. Noticing one day the temporary wooden platform that workmen had erected while renovating some of the higher parts of the cathedral there, he had the notion that a similar sort of erection would make public hangings both more efficient and more visible to spectators, thus improving their moral effectiveness. He put the innovation into immediate use in his own jurisdiction, and published a pamphlet arguing that the Scaffold execution platform was 'merciful to the offender and edifying to the populace'. The device was before long taken up with enthusiasm by magistrates throughout the country.

SOMERSAULT, Ralph c.1500–1542 English jester, noted for his acrobatic tumbling and leaping. Nothing is known of his early life, and he is first heard of performing for Cardinal Wolsey at Hampton Court in 1522. He was taken up by Henry VIII in 1529 and enjoyed the king's favour for a few years. He made the error, however, of befriending Anne Boleyn, and after her execution in 1536 took heavily to drink. Ejected by the king, he spent his last years, a pathetic figure, performing for pennies at country fairs.

'took heavily to drink'

'he can work in a good suit'

STIPPLE, Henry George 1846–1923
American painter, who in his twenties developed
the technique of painting with small dots of colour
that became better known as Pointillisme in the
hands of the French painter Georges Seurat.

Stipple devoted his own unquestionable technical skill to fashionable portrait painting, at which he made a very good living. Serious critics of the time were ungenerous to him: James McNeill Whistler said of him that 'the best thing to be said for Stipple is that he can work in a good suit without ever getting a spot of paint on it', and academic paintings of the kind he was known for were referred to as ' mere Stipples'.

STRANGLE (or **STRANGEL**), Walter c.1420–1451   Thief and murderer, born, probably, in Hamburg, whence he came in c.1445 to Greenwich, where he was employed as a sail-maker. In the years 1448–50 there were a series of horrifying murders-with-theft in Greenwich and in neighbouring parishes, in which the victims were killed by pressure of the hands upon the throat. Strangle (or Strangel) was arrested in November 1450, mainly it seems because of his foreignness and his immense physical strength, and because he had in his possession a purse for which he could not account. He confessed under examination and was executed, after a sensational trial, in January 1451.

SWIVEL, Jonathan c.1670–1728   English soldier, born in Basingstoke. He joined the Army in 1687 and fought in many of the campaigns of the Duke of Marlborough in Ireland and Flanders. In 1696 he joined a company of musketeers, but, being slight in build, found it difficult to hold the heavy weapon steady and was frequently rebuked for this by his officers. Being of a practical turn of mind, he had a blacksmith make for him an iron stand, which supported the musket firmly but allowed it to traverse freely in the horizontal plane. This greatly increased the accuracy of Swivel's fire, and he was much commended for it. (His contrivance was taken up by the Navy, but not widely used by the military until much later.)

TOUPÉE, Maurice 1801–1878   French hair-dresser, born in Beauvais. It was there, in 1843, that, concerned about his own increasing bald-

'prospered greatly under the Second Empire'

ness, he designed the male postiche that bears his name. Pleased, but also embarrassed, by the sudden improvement in his appearance, he moved to Paris, where he combined considerable success as a Lothario with a discreet service to wealthy clients. He prospered greatly under the Second Empire, but suffered a set-back during the Siege of Paris, when, it is said, several of his hairpieces were eaten in stews along with other insalubrious substances. His fortunes revived after the Peace, though it was observed that he had ceased to wear his own creations after 1871.

TRIGGER, Eli ?1739–1812 American inventor, born in New Hampshire. A Green Mountain Boy in his youth, and a remarkable shot, he is best remembered for the mechanism that revolutionized firearms towards the end of the eighteenth century. It is said that the idea came to him after he had been slow in getting off a shot at an attacking bear. Though honoured by George Washington he retired to his native mountains after the War of Independence and lived in obscurity until his death in a hunting accident.

Eli Trigger has his idea while fighting a bear

TROLLEY, Samuel 1834–1911 The inventor of
a once-familiar form of transport was born in
Seattle. His system, introduced there in 1860, was
imitated in San Francisco and then throughout
the world. The fact that this occurred without

81

'the spectacle of women drivers'

payment of royalties to himself left him in a constant state of irascibility for the rest of his life. The spectacle of women drivers in particular tended to drive him into a fury. He was institutionalized in 1901.

TROWSER, Jacob 1779–1848 English tailor, born in Clerkenwell. His tubular garments for the legs, based on cavalrymen's overalls, were regarded as a sign of insanity when he offered them for sale as civilian wear in the early 1800s, advertising them as 'Trowser's Patent Leggings: Hygienic and Economical'. He was facing bankruptcy and his wife was threatening to leave him when the Duke of Wellington wore a pair of his garments for a wager and started a fashion. Trowser made a fortune, divorced his wife and took early retirement in Brighton.

'early retirement in Brighton'

TRUNCHEON, Gabriel c.1545–1609 English peace-officer, who was employed as a constable in the City of London from 1573 until shortly before his death. A stout, jovial man, he was the first to set aside the stave or halberd normally carried by officers of the peace and to adopt instead a short, heavy staff, which he used to establish his authority with the mob and for the interrogation of suspects. He was instrumental in bringing many offenders to justice and died, greatly respected by all, during an outbreak of the plague.

VERTIGO, Giovanni (formerly Juan) c.1390–1469 Acrobat, probably of Spanish origin, who first appeared in Italy as a public performer in c.1410. Among the many other tumblers and mountebanks of the time he distinguished himself by performing at great heights, so as to add both danger and visibility to his act. His walk on a sloping tightrope from the top of the tower at Pisa to the roof of the Baptistery there

Vertigo

84

gained him both money and fame, until it was brought to an end by the ecclesiastical authorities after learned doctors had pronounced that the feelings of giddiness brought on by the mere sight of his performance were injurious to health, and probably sinful.

WALKMAN™, Otis P. 1823–1887 American inventor, born in Greenwich, Connecticut. A prolific inventor from his youth, he is best known for his development of a portable wire-recording playback device. Unfortunately, the technology available at the time was such that the device had to be pulled behind the wearer on a small wheeled cart. Walkman was a man born before his time, and it was many years after his death before technological developments enabled the device to be made truly portable.

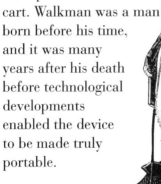

'born before his time'

von Wink

WINK, Friedrich von 1755–1811 German nobleman, born in Streltzau, Bavaria. As Bavarian ambassador to the court of King George III he introduced into London society his native custom of closing one eye to indicate that a witty or ironic remark was being made. This enjoyed a considerable vogue among the younger members of the nobility for several months. Condemned by Beau Brumell as ill-bred, it nonetheless passed into common currency, and has survived among the middle and lower classes.